BOBBY
THE PLAIN-FACED CATTLE DOG

Amy Curran

DEDICATION

To Bobby

who is picked on because of his 'plain face' but who shows me every day that it is what is inside that counts, and I hope my Children, and all other Children who meet him or read this book, will see that too.

Bobby the Plain-Faced Cattle Dog
ISBN: 978-0-6482393-1-4 Amazon

A Tales of Tails Early Reader

Published in Australia by
PINK COFFEE PUBLISHING
PO Box 483, Oberon NSW 2787
www.pinkcoffeepublishing.com

Text and Illustrations copyright Amy Curran 2018
All Rights Reserved

National Library of Australia Cataloguing-in-Publication entry information can be found at www.nla.gov.au

A guide to EARLY READER levels

A first reader, short sentences and limited amount of text on each page. Less than 750 words. Age range to 6 years old.

Sentences become a little longer, and paragraphs are introduced. Bigger words. Less than 1500 words. Age range to 8 years old.

These books are for readers ready to be independant. Contain Chapters, and more complex words. Age range to 10 years old.

The level of each book can be identified by the number, and colour of the banner, on the cover.

Bobby was so sad to leave his mum, Peggy.
Some of his brothers and sisters had already gone to new homes, but Bobby didn't want to go.
He was just a puppy.

Peggy consoled him with licks.

"Soon," she said, "you will find friends and be accepted by others."

Bobby did not understand what his mother meant by "accepted by others."

The next day, a man arrived in a noisy truck.

He had a big hat and smelt like cows.

Bobby had only seen cows from a distance, but he could smell things so far away.

He loved to smell things.

The man picked
Bobby up and plonked
him on the front seat
of the truck.

Off they went, the old
truck spluttering and
bouncing along the
road.

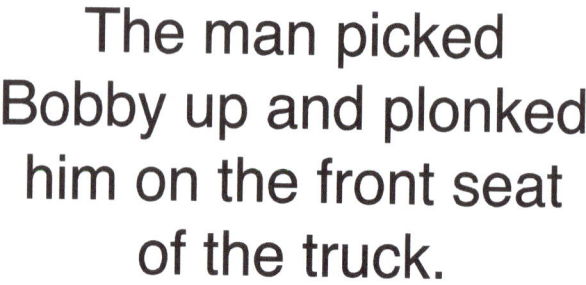

Soon they arrived at a big wooden barn that was surrounded by huge grass fields and trees.

Bobby had never seen so much grass.

"There ya go, fella,"
said the man
as he left Bobby near a
bale of hay to settle in.

Bobby could smell some other dogs close by. He peered out around the door of the barn.

Sure enough,
there were other dogs!

Bobby got excited.

The other dogs looked over at him, but didn't come over.

They just kept playing out in the field.

Bobby was wagging his tail, ready to play, but they just looked at him strangely.

He looked at the other dogs. They all looked the same.

The beautiful patches on their faces and the way they moved,
they were all the same as the dogs where he had come from.

Bobby cried as he walked back into the barn.

He wondered why the other dogs didn't want to play with him.

Bobby felt so lonely.

Bobby knew he walked the same way, barked the same way, and even played fetch the way they did.

Why didn't they want to be his friend?

"Hey, don't be sad doggy," Dally the duck quacked as she walked past Bobby with her duckings.

She was going down to the little stream that ran through the farm.

Bobby jumped in surprise!

The duck had spoken to him!

"My name is not doggy, it is Bobby. I am an Australian Cattle Dog," Bobby replied.

Dally pointed her wing towards the other dogs.

They are Australian Cattle Dogs too, but you look different. Are you sure you are a Cattle Dog?

Bobby was confused.

"Of course! I am from Australia," Bobby replied, raising his paw up with pride.

"If you say so. Follow me. Let me show you something."

The duck quacked and was soon on her way.

Bobby trailed behind.

Soon they were beside a little stream. The water appeared calm as both Bobby and the duck stared into it.

OH NO!

Bobby did look different to the other dogs!

His face was totally plain.

No patch or spot of any kind on it.

Where were his patches?

Had he lost them?

Why didn't he have any patches?

At that moment,
one of the little ducklings
fell into the stream!

A current swept up the little
duckling and started to
carry it away.

The little duckling cried for help!

Dally the mother duck was frantic and flapping her wings.

SPLASH!

Bobby didn't hesitate.

In he went!

The other dogs heard the noise and came running over.

When they reached the stream, they saw Bobby emerge from the water, soaking wet.

What was that in his mouth?

Bobby had saved the little ducking!

He placed the little bird on the ground as gently as he could, and gave a big shake.

The other dogs looked on in amazement.

Bobby was a hero!

Bobby wasn't different from them after all, even though his face was plain.

He was brave and strong, and he cared about the other animals on the farm.

It didn't matter at all that he looked different.

All the dogs who hadn't played with him gathered around and cheered for him.

They were so sorry that they had stayed away from him, just because he looked different.

Bobby was overwhelmed with pride, and so happy to be with his new friends.

He was always the same Bobby on the inside, and now they could all see that too.

Bobby

www.ingramcontent.com/pod-product-compliance
Lightning Source LLC
Chambersburg PA
CBHW042052290426
44110CB00001B/37